First World War
and Army of Occupation
War Diary
France, Belgium and Germany

3 DIVISION
8 Infantry Brigade
Royal Irish Regiment
2nd Battalion
14 August 1914 - 31 January 1915

WO95/1421/3

The Naval & Military Press Ltd
www.nmarchive.com
Published in association with The National Archives

Published by

The Naval & Military Press Ltd

Unit 10 Ridgewood Industrial Park,

Uckfield, East Sussex,

TN22 5QE England

Tel: +44 (0) 1825 749494

www.naval-military-press.com

www.nmarchive.com

This diary has been reprinted in facsimile from the original. Any imperfections are inevitably reproduced and the quality may fall short of modern type and cartographic standards.

© **Crown Copyright**
Images reproduced by permission of The National Archives, London, England, 2015.

Contents

Document type	Place/Title	Date From	Date To
Heading	WO95/1421/3 3 Divn 8 Inf Brig 2 Bn Royal Irish Regt 1914 Aug 1915 Feb		
War Diary	Southampton	14/08/1914	14/08/1914
War Diary	Boulogne	15/08/1914	15/08/1914
War Diary	Aulnoye	16/08/1914	16/08/1914
War Diary	Taisnieres	16/08/1914	20/08/1914
War Diary	St Remy	21/08/1914	21/08/1914
War Diary	Bettignies	22/08/1914	22/08/1914
War Diary	Mons	23/08/1914	24/08/1914
War Diary	Amfroipret	25/08/1914	25/08/1914
War Diary	Audencourt	26/08/1914	26/08/1914
War Diary	Cutz	30/08/1914	30/08/1914
War Diary	Courtieux	31/08/1914	31/08/1914
Map	Appendix IV (B)		
Miscellaneous	Appendix V (B)		
Map	Caudry Audencourt		
War Diary	Vaumoise	01/09/1914	03/09/1914
War Diary	Iverny	03/09/1914	03/09/1914
War Diary	Previlliers	04/09/1914	05/09/1914
War Diary	Retal	06/09/1914	06/09/1914
War Diary	Hautefeuille	07/09/1914	07/09/1914
War Diary	Chauffry	08/09/1914	08/09/1914
War Diary	Orly	09/09/1914	10/09/1914
War Diary	Chezy	11/09/1914	11/09/1914
War Diary	Ouchy-La-Ville	12/09/1914	12/09/1914
War Diary	Braine	13/09/1914	13/09/1914
War Diary	Vially	15/09/1914	25/09/1914
War Diary	Courcelles	26/09/1914	30/09/1914
Map	Appendix XIV		
War Diary	Long St Marie	05/10/1914	05/10/1914
War Diary	Amiens	05/10/1914	05/10/1914
War Diary	Noyelles	06/10/1914	06/10/1914
War Diary	Le Titre	07/10/1914	09/10/1914
War Diary	Raye	10/10/1914	10/10/1914
War Diary	Tangry	11/10/1914	13/10/1914
War Diary	Vielle Chapelle	13/10/1914	13/10/1914
War Diary	Dawn	14/10/1914	14/10/1914
War Diary	Vielle Chapelle	15/10/1914	15/10/1914
War Diary	Le Pouicke	18/10/1914	18/10/1914
War Diary	Le Riez	19/10/1914	19/10/1914
War Diary	Le Pilly	19/10/1914	20/10/1914
War Diary	St Omer	24/10/1914	31/01/1915
Miscellaneous	8th Infty Bde Bn Royal Irish Regt		
Map	Action At Le Riez And Le Pilly		
Miscellaneous	Appendix XXX		
Miscellaneous	Appendix XXXI		
Miscellaneous	Appendix XXXII		

WO 95 1421/3

3 DIVN
8 INF BRIG
2 BN. ROYAL IRISH REGT
1914 AUG – 1915 FEB

WAR DIARY
INTELLIGENCE SUMMARY.
(Erase heading not required.)

Army Form C. 2118.

Instructions regarding War Diaries and Intelligence Summaries are contained in F. S. Regs., Part II. and the Staff Manual respectively. Title pages will be prepared in manuscript.

Hour, Date, Place	Summary of Events and Information	Remarks and references to Appendices
5.15 a.m. Fri. Aug. 14th. SOUTHAMPTON	Left Southampton. As we commenced to cross the Channel at 3 p.m. an escort of cruisers joined us and 3 #### on the North of our track, 4.10 a.m. the North. Arrived at BOULOGNE about 6 p.m. and marched to a rest camp about 3 miles distance.	
Sat. Aug. 15th. BOULOGNE	The Bn. was inspected by the French G.O.C. L.O.C. Left camp at 6.45 p.m. and entrained at 10 p.m. for unknown destination.	
4 a.m. Sun. Aug. 16th. AULNOYE	Arrived at AULNOYE about 2 miles from the Belgium frontier & detrained. Marched about 3 miles to TAISNIERES. When we went into billets. We received orders that patrols were to be sent to ANDERSON with 12 men remained at AULNOYE railway station in duty along the business of them into billets, but shall improve with experience.	

Army Form C. 2118.

WAR DIARY
or
INTELLIGENCE SUMMARY.

(Erase heading not required.)

Instructions regarding War Diaries and Intelligence Summaries are contained in F. S. Regs., Part II. and the Staff Manual respectively. Title pages will be prepared in manuscript.

Hour, Date, Place	Summary of Events and Information	Remarks and references to Appendices
10. a.m. Sun Aug 16th. TAISNIERES	Over 30 British aeroplanes passed over us as we were on the march to our billets.	
Monday, Aug. 17th. TAISNIERES.	Route march under Coy arrangements. Reviewed & man inspected our billets	
Tuesday, Aug. 18th. TAISNIERES.	Bn. went march of about 7 miles in the morning. Nothing remarkable and everything satisfactory. Coy. arrangements in the afternoon. Many men have sore and defective feet. We heard to-day with great regret of the death of Lt. Wolfenden, our Army Corps Commander A.C.	
Wednesday, Aug. 19th. TAISNIERES.	Coys. at disposal of Coy Commanders — practice of attack. Divisional payment in the field & medals to Coys. It takes 2½ hours to pay out 5 hrs a man. Not at all satisfactory. The system is impossible — the Captains signature is the only safe guard against chaotic confusion	

WAR DIARY
or
INTELLIGENCE SUMMARY
(Erase heading not required.)

Army Form C. 2118.

Instructions regarding War Diaries and Intelligence Summaries are contained in F. S. Regs, Part II. and the Staff Manual respectively. Title pages will be prepared in manuscript.

Hour, Date, Place	Summary of Events and Information	Remarks and References to Appendices
Wednesday Aug. 19th. TAISNIERES.	We heard through the A.S.C. that we move to ST REMY. and form there do a 24 hours march further forward. Evidently the A.S.C. are somewhat in means of giving away information as to —	YY
Thursday Aug. 20th. TAISNIERES. 9.45 a.m.	Marched out and billeted at ST REMY. (my host billets. The L.O. now called Coy. Comdr.) and addressed them on the following points:— 1) All men to be kept in coy billets. 2) Coys. to be prepared to fall in at short notice. 3) Early information of casualties required at after an action. Unless noticed at 11 a.m. for march out 5.40 a.m. tomorrow.	YY

WAR DIARY
or
INTELLIGENCE SUMMARY

(Erase heading not required.)

Army Form C. 2118.

Hour, Date, Place	Summary of Events and Information	Remarks and References to Appendices
Friday, Aug. 21st. St. REMY.	Orders received at 2.a.m. advancing the hour of march by half-an-hour. Marched at 5.15 a.m. "A" Coy advance Guard "B" Coy at head of main body. We passed the Middlesex Regt, Gordons, & R. Scots en route. Arrived at BETTIGNIES via MAUBERGE at mid-day. Royal Irish and the Middlesex billeted at BETTIGNIES. The other two battalions at GOGNIES. The H.Q. Coy at latter place and Bde. Hd. Qrs. at former. Lieut ANDERSON with men who had been standing duty at AULNOYE railway station rejoined the Regt.	

WAR DIARY
INTELLIGENCE SUMMARY
(Erase heading not required.)

Army Form C. 2118.

Instructions regarding War Diaries and Intelligence Summaries are contained in F. S. Regs., Part II. and the Staff Manual respectively. Title pages will be prepared in manuscript.

Hour, Date, Place	Summary of Events and Information	Remarks and References to Appendices
Saturday Aug 22nd BETTIGNIES.	Moved Northwards & ordered to hold line NOUVELLES – HARVENG – HAVAY joining eastwards. Later orders were received to hold line, and junction at FAUBG BARTHELEMY (just east of MONS.) – HARMIGNIES – GIVRY. Middex holding northern portion, R.S. The northern part.	
	5pm. Regt was ordered to hold ST SYMPHORIEN. and VILLERS ST GHISLAIN, while Middlesex were detailed to hold canal bridges:- (i) Immediately North of NIMY. (ii) Lock No. 5. (iii) Near OBURG STATION.	
6.15 pm	MAJOR S.E. ST LEGER with "A" Bart (A+C Coys) proceeded to VILLERS ST GHISLAIN, relieved the Cavalry Brigade throughout the night with help of a Coy R.E., placed the village in a state of defence. Gen. HAMILTON met MAJOR ST LEGER at the village & told him to dig himself well in.	

WAR DIARY or INTELLIGENCE SUMMARY

Army Form C. 2118.

Hour, Date, Place	Summary of Events and Information	Remarks and References to Appendices
MONS 23rd AUG 4.30pm	MIDDLESEX and ROYAL IRISH retired from forward position to position in front of Hosp (see sketch) on left of GORDON HIGHLANDERS. NOUVELLES	APPENDIX IV & see sketch - where this was attempted shown
5.30 pm	MIDDLESEX continued their retirement on ROYAL IRISH ordered to gain touch with GORDONS & Enemy following up very closely prevented this being carried out - Bng Gen DORAN now ordered retirement to be continued - further purposes indicated by Hardly attacking GORDON HIGHLANDERS and R.I.M. SCOTS who were leaving MONS HARMIGNIES road	
7 pm	D Coy reinforced GORDON HIGHLANDERS - B Coy took up a position to reinforce it.	
8.0 pm	Ordered to retreat with Guns to Ciply NOUVELLES	
10.0 pm	Guns were handled to road & retirement to ... carried out - arrived about midnight preceded with 50 men returned with Major DANIEL who had obtained permission to Major ...... to find his Guns which had temporary abandoned than was eventually ...... out - MAJOR DANIELL rejoining regiment at about 4.30am	
24 August 4.30am	Lt Col COX got separated from his unit soon after our action at MONS and MAJR St LEGER Commanding unit the retreat to offensive Col COX rejoined the Regt ...... NOUVELLES	For Casualties at MONS see APPENDIX V

Army Form C. 2118.

WAR DIARY
INTELLIGENCE SUMMARY
(Erase heading not required.)

Instructions regarding War Diaries and Intelligence Summaries are contained in F.S. Regs., Part II. and the Staff Manual respectively. Title pages will be prepared in manuscript.

Hour, Date, Place	Summary of Events and Information	Remarks and References to Appendices
Mon. Aug. 24th 8 a.m.	Retired via BOUGNIES and GENLY.	*Neiit N.C.C. HARMON reported Batt at about 1.0 pm reported missing. Rumour Sleger, who placed him temporarily in command of H Coy, when he have had no news.
9.15 a.m.	Bn. took up a position about 1 mile south of GENLY with Gordon Highlanders on their right	
3.0 pm	[illegible text about Gordons moving to Bois du Vieux - H.'s Company retired to help X Coy of the Gordon Highlanders.] Cross B' Sketch APPENDIX V	
	N.B. Under slight artillery fire. No Casualties	
	AMFROIPRET.	
4 p.m.	Retired through BAVAI to AMFROIPRET arriving about 10 p.m. & Bn. bivouacked in a small field. Here supplies were received but no the cooks wagon was lost at MONS, there was no means of cooking.	
Tues. Aug. 25th 5 a.m. AMFROIPRET.	Continued retirement via WARGNIES LE PETIT — LE QUESNOY — ROMERIES — SOLESMES — VIESLY — CAUDRY to AUDENCOURT.	Y
4 p.m.	Bn. reached CAUDRY & halted in a large field to cook tea in some buckets & cans that had been requisitioned en route.	
5 p.m.	Very heavy rain drenched everybody	
6.30 p.m.	Moved to billets at AUDENCOURT, "B" Coy furnishing two piquet on the eastern side of the village.	

Army Form C. 2118.

WAR DIARY
of
INTELLIGENCE SUMMARY
(Erase heading not required.)

Instructions regarding War Diaries and Intelligence Summaries are contained in F. S. Regs., Part II. and the Staff Manual respectively. Title pages will be prepared in manuscript.

Hour, Date, Place		Summary of Events and Information	Remarks and References to Appendices
AUDENCOURT Wed. 26th Aug	3.Am	B" stood to arms until 5.am	
	6.Am	Enemy commenced to open shell fire on the guns in position in W of the village & retire fire gradually increased in intensity.	
	9.30 Am	In reports to a request for support before the German Hdqrs on the left of his entrenchment, CYD Coy proceeded under Major S.E. St LEGER and occupied positions shown on the sketch	APPENDIX IX
	9.35 Am	D Coy under Major E.H DANIELL D.S.O was sent to the road cutting 500° S.W of the village to report to GENERAL HAMILTON (comd of 3rd Div) who directed him to report to Brig Gen. McCRACKEN Com of 7th Inf Bde at CAUDRY. This Coy was distributed as shown on sketch	
	2.30 pm	Major DANIELL having collected unknown details returned to this position S.W of AUDENCOURT/shown by a dotted red line on sketch	
	4.45 pm	Orders to retire were given and AUDENCOURT was evacuated — This order was not received by Major St LEGER who remained in position.	
	6.30 pm	Capt ELLIOT finding that his left flank was threatened by a German advance from CAUDRY directed Lieut E.M. PHILLIPS with a platoon to retire. This officer with a few men reached Major St LEGER's position but was almost immediately wounded	

WAR DIARY
or
INTELLIGENCE SUMMARY
(Erase heading not required.)

Army Form C. 2118.

Hour, Date, Place	Summary of Events and Information	Remarks and References to Appendices
AUDENCOURT 26th AUG 6.30 am	Capt ELLIOT had received no orders to retire. MAJOR SLEGER was now driven from his position by a heavy M.G. fire from his right front (i.e. right rear (at about 150 x range) & directed men in right rear (at about 150 x range) & directed men also to attempt to reach in position reached by remainder of "C" Coy under MAJOR E.M. PANTER DOWNES. MAJOR SLEGER wounded in right arm reached Major PANTER DOWNES at dusk but found this Officer mortally wounded himself in the stomach had directed his Coy now without Officers to try to retire through the birchfields in which was the trench gap left open by the enemy. Few Notices account see APPENDIX VI + VII. All the 1st line Transport under mand on the day I was incapacitated. AUDENCOURT during the area of very heavy bombardment sustained during the whole of this day that the damage by high explosives in the day I R of W box was no wounded early in the day & MAJOR SLEGER being wounded Rearming the command of the Battalion devolved on MAJOR DANIELL to BEAUREVOIR. The battalion arriving about 11.pm went into billets. Recommendations submitted by hand at 5/10/14.	APPENDIX VI + VII For Casualties at CAUDRY see APPENDIX X For Transport of supples 23-3 Aug see APPENDIX XI see APPENDIX XII

Army Form C. 2118.

WAR DIARY
of
INTELLIGENCE SUMMARY.
(Erase heading not required.)

Instructions regarding War Diaries and Intelligence Summaries are contained in F. S. Regs., Part II. and the Staff Manual respectively. Title pages will be prepared in manuscript.

Hour, Date, Place	Summary of Events and Information	Remarks and references to Appendices
Sunday. Aug. 30th 5.15 a.m.	Continued retirement with four hour halt in middle of day. Weather very hot.	W
CUTZ 6 p.m.	Billetted in school at COURTIEUX where train joined Bn.	W
Mon. Aug. 31st. 3.30 a.m.	Train left.	
7 a.m.	Bn. left with orders to proceed via POTINGRON	
COURTIEUX.	– PI DE POUY – MORTE FONTAINE – TAILLÉ FONTAINE – EMÉVILLE – FEIGNEUX, & DUVY. Orders were changed on march to proceed via VILLERS-COTTERETS, & VAUMOISE where Bn went on Outpost duty extending from Rwy ½ mile W. of village VAUMOISE to FONTAINIE Fm. where they joined up with 9th Bde.	W
Tues. Sept 1st 3.45 a.m. VAUMOISE.	Railway bridge blown up about 150 x W. of left outpost groups B.V.	

WAR DIARY or INTELLIGENCE SUMMARY.

(Erase heading not required.)

Army Form C. 2118

APPENDIX II

Hour, Date, Place	Summary of Events and Information	Remarks and references to Appendices
26/8	The following officers proceeded with the Battⁿ	
26/8	Lieut Col S.J.A. Cox In command	Lieut H.C.C. HARRISON Hillstaff Officer
26/8	Major S.E. STEGER 2ⁿᵈ in command	Major H.W. LONG (R.A.M.C.) Medical Officer
26/8	Lieut R.E.G. PHILLIPS Adjutant	
	Capt. J. RICHINGS Quartermaster	
	Lieut F.H.L. RUSHTON Transport Officer	
	Lieut P.J. WHITTY Machine Gun Officer	
	Lieut A.M.S. TANDY Signalling Officer	
	Lieut A.D. FRASER Scout Officer	
26/8	"A" COMPANY	"B" COMPANY
25/8	Capt. W. MELLOR	MAJOR E.H.E. DANIELL. D.S.O
25/8	Capt. I.B. GEORGE	Lieut F.G. FERGUSON
25/8	2ⁿᵈ Lieut J.D. SHINE	Lieut D.P. LAING
25/8	2ⁿᵈ Lieut C.F.T. D.B ffrench	2ⁿᵈ Lieut A.R. NEWTON-KING
25/8	2ⁿᵈ Lieut E.C. GUINNESS	
	"C" COMPANY	"D" COMPANY
25/8	Capt. & Bt Major E.M. PAINTER DOWNES	Capt. G.A. ELLIOTT	26/8 ᴀᴍ
25/8	Capt. V.S. FITZGERALD	Capt. the Hon. ᵇˡᵉ F.G.A. FORBES	27 ᴘ.ᴍ.
25/8	Lieut. A.E.B. ANDERSON	Lieut. E.M. PHILLIPS 3/13ᵗʰ	26/8 ʷ
25/8	Lieut C.B. GIBBONS	Lieut C.G. MAGRATH	26/8 ᴍ
	Officers of the Bⁿ who proceeded with Special appointments	
	Bᵗ Major C.J. BURKE } with Royal Flying Corps	
	Capt H.C. MACDONNELL }	
	Lieut H.D. HARVEY-KELLY }	
	Capt A.R.G. GORDON Staff Capt 6ᵗʰ Inf. Bde.	

APPENDIX I

WAR DIARY
2nd Bn The Royal Irish Regt.
INTELLIGENCE SUMMARY

Army Form C. 2118

Investigation went off without a hitch, except as the following particulars.

I. No travelling kitchens were available, their loss was severely felt – They were not issued till approx'd 19.11.14

II. Difficulty was experienced in obtaining ordnance stores, more especially boots of right size required.

III. The recruits were badly fitted with boots at the depot, in many cases also their serge clothing & caps had to be changed.

IV. A mass of correspondence was known on Coy officers. Had the "Batt" moved on the 8th day, it would have been quite impossible to have completed the documents to this received.

(a) The details on 75-90 Army Books 64 had not been entered correctly. The men had got separation allowances had to be filled (b) Yellow forms for separation allowance their names had to be filled in with names of wife & children in for officers

(c) Almost bomb by the name detail had to be taken down in connection with the allotment of pay (d) Wills had not been made

V.L. Meyer Major
2/P.S. Regt.

MONS AUG 23rd 1914

Showing the successive positions taken up by the 2 Bn ROYAL IRISH REGT.

APPENDIX IV (B)

True N

German attack

Uhlans debouching from here suffered severely from our M.G

Enclosed poor field of fire

The 4/MIDDLESEX apparently held position S of river

Enclosed
C Co
½ B Co
A Co
D Co

To OBOURG 1½ m
D Co advanced 1½ hrs

Quarry
Cemetery
Hosp
Enclosed
1 Platoon B Co

M.G. 1st Position
To HAVRE (2½ m)

MONS

Faub. Barthelemy
Cabbage patch
Plough
2nd Position A & C Coys
Potato Field
Hosp
B Co
2nd Position B Co

M.G. 3rd Position one gun put out of action & abandoned

Regtl Q.M. Sgt Fitzpatrick & 40 men held trench here until 11.0 pm

M.G. 2nd & 4th position second gun put out of action

Section R.F.A

Battn reorganized here 5.15 pm

German Inf here at 6.0 pm

B Co sent up here to get touch with GORDON Highlanders

3rd Position
A Co
C Co
B Co

Artillery position believed to have been here

HYON

Gordon Highrs under Col Neish
German attack 7-8 pm
40 Bde R.F.A
D Co Royal Irish
GORDON HIGHLANDERS

Open grass B Co
A & C Coy
Enclosed
Guns temporarily abandoned

4th Position
Swampy ground

German Inf followed up to here

Retirement carried out at dusk & then head to NOUVELLES

Royal Scots

S.S. St Leger Major
2/ Royal Irish Regt

Mile 1 — ¾ — ½ — ¼ — 0
Scale approx.

The positions of the GORDON HIGHLANDERS and ROYAL SCOTS is only approx.

APPENDIX IV(B)

APPENDIX IV(B)

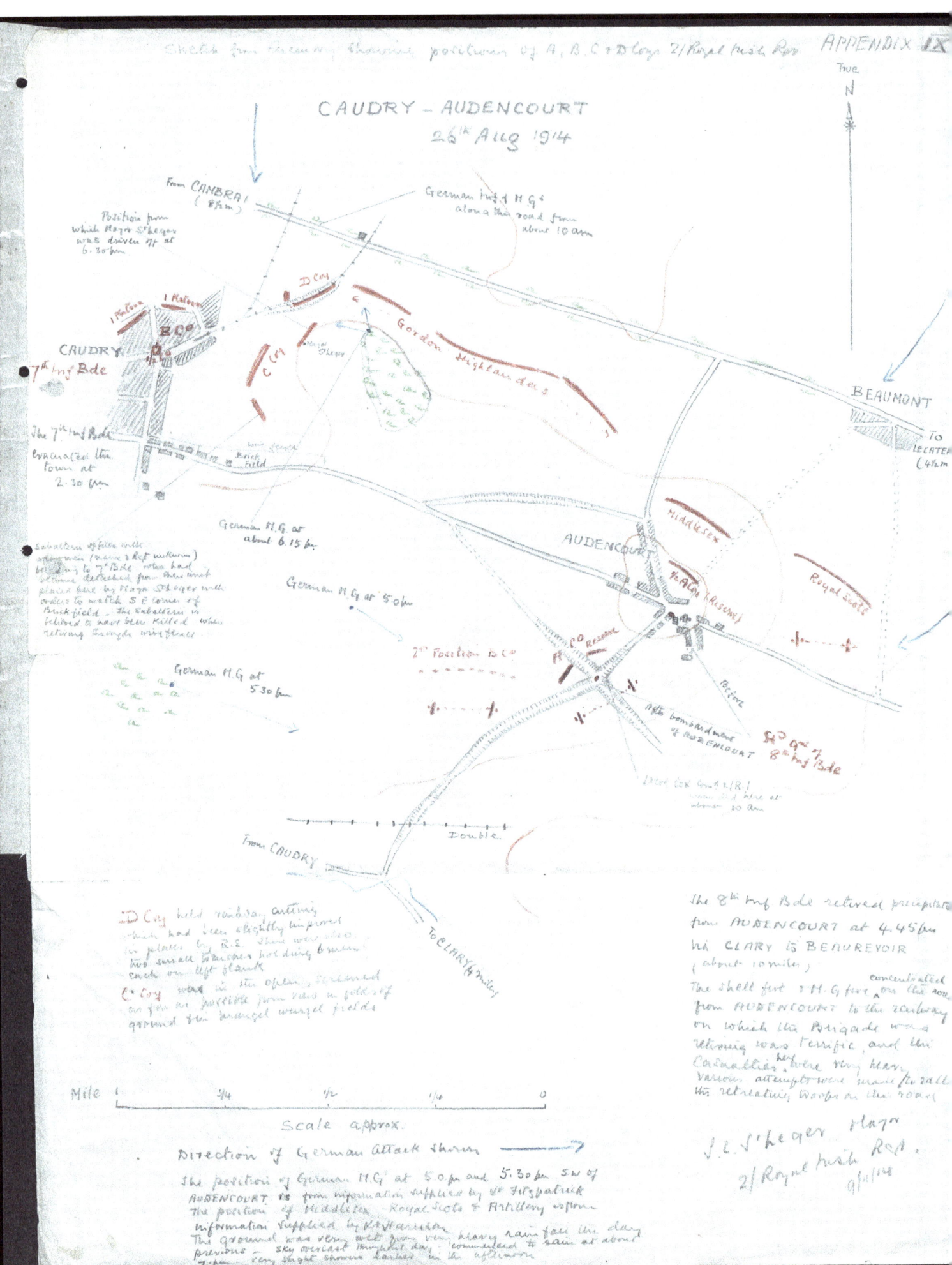

2nd R. Suss. Regt.   8/7   2 ₮

WAR DIARY
of
INTELLIGENCE SUMMARY
(Erase heading not required.)

SEPT. 1, 1914

Army Form C. 2118.

Hour, Date, Place	Summary of Events and Information	Remarks and References to Appendices
Sun. Sept 1st 1:45 am VAUMOISE	Railway bridge blown up about 150 x N Lefranfort junch.	
9:30 am	Retirement continued reaching via LEVIGNEN →FRESNOY → VILLERS → ST GENEST and billet at CHEVREVILLE.	
Mon. Sept 2nd 3.15 a.m.	Retirement continuing further & orders were issued by columns & proceeded to billet to at MONTMYON arriving at IVERNY about 2 hours at midday	
Tues. Sept 3rd 7 am	Retirement continued with orders to march via PENCHARD → MEAUX → BOUTIGNY → ST FIACRE → VILLENAREVIL → NEUFM.... PROVI... SIGNY → SIGNETS. Orders were changed during march. 2nd Bn billetted at VANCIEN TRIL	

$9-26-6)$ W 257-996 100,000 1/12 HWV   79/5298

WAR DIARY
INTELLIGENCE SUMMARY
(Erase heading not required.)

Army Form C. 2118.

Instructions regarding War Diaries and Intelligence Summaries are contained in F. S. Regs., Part II. and the Staff Manual respectively. Title pages will be prepared in manuscript.

Hour, Date, Place	Summary of Events and Information	Remarks and References to Appendices
2nd Sept 2nd Army 1/9/17	Royal Irish & Seaforth Highlanders furnishing outposts from LE PEST LOUP to Ym BEAUBRY. 5th Barrow left 9th Barrow right of R.I. General line run S. of PREVILLE.	
7 p.m.	German aeroplane passed over outpost position. Fire was opened on it without success. Machine was afterwards brought down by artillery. Damaged fast was forwarded with PREVILLIERS during night.	W
2nd Sept. 6.30 A.M. 2/9/17 PREVILLIERS	Germans attacked on VANCOURTOIS & X road to with NW of MONTGODFRY was met on in St LACHAPELLE. The attack was by 2nd Brigade failed to reach the ridge	W

WAR DIARY
or
INTELLIGENCE SUMMARY
(Erase heading not required.)

Army Form C. 2118.

Instructions regarding War Diaries and Intelligence Summaries are contained in F. S. Regs., Part II. and the Staff Manual respectively. Title pages will be prepared in manuscript.

Hour, Date, Place	Summary of Events and Information	Remarks and References to Appendices
Sat Sept 5th 7 a.m.	March continued all night. Bn reached RETAL when 6th Bde Brigade went into billets. Ye en billd in _____ in _____ for breakfast at Retal, and _____ _____ _____ _____ _____ _____ _____ able to _____ _____ _____ since the battle of MONS.	
Same	Some returned voluntarily to arms. (no _____) Inspection who were in change of the party _____ _____ _____ before leaving the base.	
12 Midnight	Indications were received of an advance of the British Army.	
Sun Sept 6th 8.30 am	Dawn announced nearer. RETAL. 7 am _____ on reaching NEUFMOUTIERS, men _____ had any breakfast 1st Brigade marched from OBEL ISQUE to made to En FORESIDE- CRECY about 7 P.M.	

WAR DIARY
INTELLIGENCE SUMMARY
(Erase heading not required.)

Army Form C. 2118.

Hour, Date, Place	Summary of Events and Information	Remarks and References to Appendices
Sep 5th. 8 am. 1 mile North of CREVECOEUR. PITRE (1st MIDD)	Commenced march (Advanced guard) to CREVECOEUR via LA HOUSSIETTE	
1.30 p.m.	The Brigade was ordered to LES MESNIERS where it was understood the enemy was in a small wood out to the West of our flanks. Orders for the attack were to march all night to try and cut off German Left flank at SIGNY LA MARNE	
2.30 p.m.	Marched to CREVECOEUR where two halts were made.	
6.30 p.m.	Marched to HAUTEFEUILLE where a billet was found in a School near the 4th Middlesex.	

WAR DIARY
INTELLIGENCE SUMMARY

(Erase heading not required.)

Army Form C. 2118.

Hour, Date, Place	Summary of Events and Information	Remarks and References to Appendices
Mon Sept 4th HERLEVILLE	It was reported that the advance would be continued about 8 a.m. but as there was no news of the Brigade on our right, the battalion did not take place till 9 am. Scouts left in advance of at the head of the Column and screens of fours to R. & L. Shortly after a breeze of long grass and thistles, what many of the men thought were Germans, the Column was checked about ½ an hour while this was investigated. The march was continued until the Battn arrived not come into action.	Information received last night 2nd Sept.
Sep 1st [illegible]	[illegible] Four Companies were billeted in village. Bn HdQrs at Lieut. D. Fourcault's Forces de Chauffry	

Signed [illegible]
Forces de Chauffry

WAR DIARY
or
INTELLIGENCE SUMMARY
(Erase heading not required.)

Army Form C. 2118.

Hour, Date, Place	Summary of Events and Information	Remarks and References to Appendices
14th Aug 8 AM 1914 CHAUFFRY	Royal Irish formed [illeg.] of the advanced guard to the Brigade, with 8th Hussars on our left & 14th Brigade on our right. 9.15 AM Infantry in contact with enemy near [illeg.] about 2 miles North of REBAIS. 4th Batn. & Dismtd Guard formed the van. Took up a strong position in a valley between ORLY and BUSSEROLE. Enemy about 1,000 [illeg.] to our front, supported by artillery. Sent 2 coys to contest the village of [illeg.] & B.G.[?] Coys. had retired to more [illeg.] [illeg.] ORLY and BUSSEROLE to CITRY. Enemy nearby and pressing the enemy. [illeg.] 5th Bde only [illeg.] ORLY [illeg.] [illeg.] [illeg.] For details see Report (Action at ORLY APPENDIX XIII — CASUALTIES APPENDIX XV	N See sketch APPENDIX XIV See APPENDICES XIII and XV

WAR DIARY
or
INTELLIGENCE SUMMARY

(Erase heading not required.)

Army Form C. 2118.

Instructions regarding War Diaries and Intelligence Summaries are contained in F. S. Regs., Part II. and the Staff Manual respectively. Title pages will be prepared in manuscript.

Hour, Date, Place	Summary of Events and Information	Remarks and References to Appendices
Sun. Sept. 6th CHAUFFRY	On leaving the Bivouac after the battle along the Enemy's forward line, reinforcements (little being gathered in) 81 of the morning from MOISY CHOISY gathered, moving on. Fire amongst the the Enemy up the Tkapferens & 636 there.	x Lieut D. FOULKES
Mon. Sept. 7th ORLY T.R.DAY	than left at 9.0 am, marched as army Rte RAY via BUSSIERES-LEFERONCOURT-NANCY - NANTEAU to LIZY at CROUTES. rather rain, but night and hot sun. Arr. 10.p.m.	
16.30 hrs	were gathered. Left our new outfit to PARIS did not exhaust us long. they had to march to Paris about whole war of MARNE.	M/N
7. h/30	flood about at LIZY	

WAR DIARY
or
INTELLIGENCE SUMMARY
(Erase heading not required.)

Army Form C. 2118.

Hour, Date, Place	Summary of Events and Information	Remarks and References to Appendices
Thurs. Sept. 10th 5.30 a.m.	Bde. left at 5.30 a.m., 8th Bde. forming an advance to Brel. Cav. Bde. was instructed to proceed to about 1 mile N. of CROUTES. The advance was continued along the line via BEZU-LE-GUERY ~ MARIGNY-EN-ORXOIS ~ VEUILLY ~ VINLY and CHEZY which they reached about 6 p.m. The Brigade did not come into action though the rest of the Div. were engaged most of the day, capturing about two howitzers of 3 in., 10th, & 9th Corps. The Royal Scots formed a forward screen about 5½ of the advance guard 4 Officers of the 9th Jäger, the prisoners were billetted in church. Lieut. Landy (TANDY) & Haltam forming a guard while the Four officers dined, slept and had breakfast at the left passing morning with officers R. S.	W

WAR DIARY
or
INTELLIGENCE SUMMARY

(Erase heading not required.)

Army Form C. 2118.

Instructions regarding War Diaries and Intelligence Summaries are contained in F. S. Regs., Part II. and the Staff Manual respectively. Title pages will be prepared in manuscript.

Hour, Date, Place	Summary of Events and Information	Remarks and References to Appendices
Fri Sept 11th. 5 a.m.	Had orders to be ready to move at 5 a.m.	
CHEZY. 7.45 a.m.	Brigade eventually moved with orders to proceed via DAMMARD — NEUILLY — VICHEL — OULCHY — LA – VILLE, GRAND ROZOY, 9th Bde forming advanced guard	
	Brought forward along in rear of Bn. with intention of leaving them at NEUILLY station but discovered that Railway had been blown up at a tunnel, so we continued with reference to billets at OUCHY-LA-VILLE which was reached at about 2.30 p.m.	
Sat Sept 12th 6 a.m. OUCHY-LA-VILLE.	Left & proceeded via COURDOUX — LAUNOY — MAAL to billets at BRAINE. On nearing BRAINE at 6 p.m. found we were called to arms as 5th Cav Bde. but were now called to arms action.	

Army Form C. 2118.

WAR DIARY
INTELLIGENCE SUMMARY
(Erase heading not required.)

Instructions regarding War Diaries and Intelligence Summaries are contained in F. S. Regs., Part II. and the Staff Manual respectively. Title pages will be prepared in manuscript.

Hour, Date, Place	Summary of Events and Information	Remarks and References to Appendices
Sept. 13th 5 p.m. OUCHY-LA-VILLE	Before leaving OUCHY-LA-VILLE Armoured Cars handed over to London Highlanders. There was heavy engagements all day on both our flanks (our advanced guard (19th Brigade) was only slightly opposed	

Army Form C. 2118.

WAR DIARY
or
INTELLIGENCE SUMMARY
(Erase heading not required.)

Instructions regarding War Diaries and Intelligence Summaries are contained in F. S. Regs., Part II. and the Staff Manual respectively. Title pages will be prepared in manuscript.

Hour, Date, Place	Summary of Events and Information	Remarks and References to Appendices
6.30 13.9.14 BRAINE	Marched at 6.30 a.m. Kept the Berkshires ahead of us our (advance) Brigade being Rear Guard	
8.30 a.m.	On emerging from AIGUIENNE wood 1 mile south of CHASSEMY Brigade came under artillery fire from high ground near CHIVRES north of river AISNE. Battalion moved in single file into (artillery formation?) ... took cover two companies ... Berkshires (?) on ... Norfolks (?) ... ground ... that ... we ... on ... the night.	
	account by Lieut F.H.L. RUSHTON APPENDIX XV APPENDIX XVI	J.Y.
	on the AISNE	
1.30 p.m.	Received orders from VAILLY westward to ... sections ... being ... sent ...	
2.30	across & reached ... freeing ...	
11.30	... at (?) ... to position in high ground E of S' PIERRE	
6.0 P.M.	B Company took up position on high ground N of VAILLY. Rest of Battalion of Royal Berks moved more before us and occupied high ground in between their two position. Battalion billeted in S' PIERRE	

WAR DIARY
or
INTELLIGENCE SUMMARY
(Erase heading not required.)

Army Form C. 2118.

Instructions regarding War Diaries and Intelligence Summaries are contained in F. S. Regs., Part II. and the Staff Manual respectively. Title pages will be prepared in manuscript.

Hour, Date, Place	Summary of Events and Information	Remarks and References to Appendices
3am 15th Sept Vieuil	In advance of the General line heavy shelled bridge throughout the night. Return march at night.	
6 am	Packmen sent to serve	
11.29 am	Heavy french brigade coming up in to attack the day very hot. Rifle & heavy french brigade gallant at night.	
	Gunners with another unsuccessful attack on north western frontier very heavy infantry on our left all day about all night very cold	
3 a.m. 16th Sept	Stood to arms artillery engagements continue	
8 am	Regiment went to VIANY by half companies to two farms each to day for drinking half A Company were caught by artillery fire on return journey casualties 5 wounded	
4 Pm	Very heavy artillery fire opened on our position with high explosives - cavalry & several 15 pounder stood from on our position & horses up by nights and ammunition returned	

WAR DIARY
INTELLIGENCE SUMMARY

Army Form C. 2118.

Hour, Date, Place	Summary of Events and Information	Remarks and References to Appendices
3 AM 17 Sept. VAULX	Stood to arms. Awaiting fire continued and 3 men were wounded withdrawn from night dispositions. 1st day. Enemy artillery fire was severe in the night but was almost directly stopped. but there was a large bomb amount and to typist arrival —	'x' Captain H.G. Gregoire " W.J. Parris England 3" 2nd Lieut J.R. Rossington 3" " " D.S. Smyth " " " P.E.N. Howard 2" " " W.H. Flynn 3" "
6 PM 17 Sept	Awaiting fire was changed so no return proceeding to night dispositions. No excess army made to effect relief withdrew night dispositions and stood to arms.	
3 AM 18 Sept	Stood to arms.	
	Awaiting fire opened less awaiting fire but some prepared during fires on our support many hours. Heavy MG material but very long range. Recommendations forwarded by Major DANIELL APPENDIX XVII	APPENDIX XVII
3 AM 19 Sept	Stood to arms — Awaiting fire continued. Usual day.	
3.15 hrs 20 Sept	Attack by enemy. The right Brigade on our right were attacked in strength during the morning but we suffered twenty casualties altogether.	

Army Form C. 2118.

WAR DIARY
or
INTELLIGENCE SUMMARY

(*Erase heading not required.*)

Instructions regarding War Diaries and Intelligence Summaries are contained in F. S. Regs., Part II. and the Staff Manual respectively. Title pages will be prepared in manuscript.

Hour, Date, Place	Summary of Events and Information	Remarks and References to Appendices
31st AUG Sept 22nd VAILLY	Short to arms. Machine guns received very little artillery fire all day but Germans continued their	"
1.30 PM	assault in night & have a	
3.15 from Sept 22	steady stream from trenches sent 6's man	"
	arrival	
23rd September	no further developments -	"
24th September	no further developments -	"
2 PM 25th	2 killed and 1 wounded by shrapnel	"
6.30 "	Relieved by Royal Fusiliers and proceeded to bivouac for rest —	
2 AM 26th Sept (UNDECIPHERED)	carried	
27th "	attacked by Garibaldi Frailon	"
28 "		
29 "		
30	just growing rations and returning	

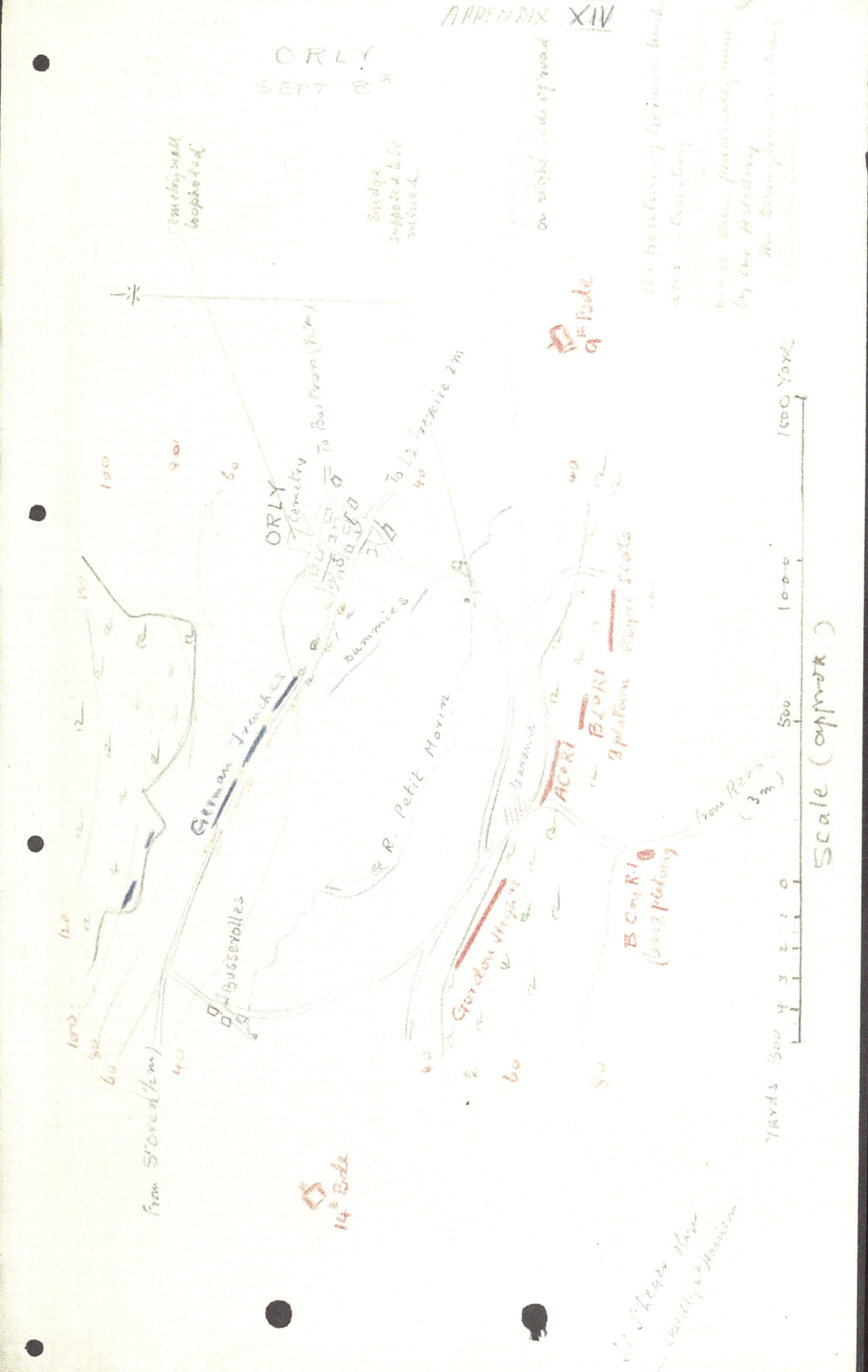

WAR DIARY
or
INTELLIGENCE SUMMARY

Army Form C. 2118.

Instructions regarding War Diaries and Intelligence Summaries are contained in F. S. Regs., Part II. and the Staff Manual respectively. Title pages will be prepared in manuscript.

(Erase heading not required.)

Hour, Date, Place	Summary of Events and Information	Remarks and References to Appendices
5.30 PM 5th Apr. King S¹ Mil.	"B" Company advised half of tomorrow's movement.	
7.30	Draw arms and dismiss unknown.	
12 m	Arrived and departed upon short halt, and were informed our destination was CALAIS	
6 am 6th NOYELLES	Arrived	
3. PM 7th LE TITRE	Detrained and arrived at LE TITRE at 7 Pm	
8 " "		
2 AM 9th	Left for RUE	
1 am 10th RUE	Arrived	
9 PM "	The order was received for all available men to muster to TANGRY transport to leave in the morning	
5 AM 11th Col. TANGRY	Battalion arrived	
5 PM "	Transport arrived.	

WAR DIARY or INTELLIGENCE SUMMARY

(Erase heading not required.)

Army Form C. 2118.

Instructions regarding War Diaries and Intelligence Summaries are contained in F.S. Regs., Part II. and the Staff Manual respectively. Title pages will be prepared in manuscript.

Hour, Date, Place	Summary of Events and Information	Remarks and references to Appendices
12th Oct 1914 TANCRY 4 P.M.	Battn as adv guard of the Brigade who reached a farm S. of Canal between HINGES and VIELLE CHAPELLE — under slight Artillery fire during advance. B & C Coys on outpost duty during the night — no signs of the enemy.	
13th Oct. 1914 6 am	The Battn in reserve proceeded to VIELLE CHAPELLE	
5 pm	Crossed the Canal S. of that place with the MIDDLESEX under shell fire but further advance was arrested by heavy fire. The GORDON HIGHLANDERS & ROYAL SCOTS crossed the Canal & forced in the left & supported them in VIELLE CHAPELLE. Casualties — Billeted at night in VIELLE CHAPELLE.	
VIELLE CHAPELLE	The town had been recently dealt with from shell fire. Several houses were on fire & the Church destroyed.	
14th Oct DAWN	Battn stood to arms at dawn. Brigade advanced for about 1 mile. The ROYAL SCOTS leading. 2nd MIDDLESEX on right GORDONS on left — ROYAL IRISH in reserve. On the heavy shell fire coming later ½ mile in the western dug trenches in rear of the line. Capt H.G. GREGORIE	
9 am	also received N.C.O.s men & men driven back & wounded. Gorden's fire very heavy. GORDON's & German fire very heavy - GORDON's reinforced by 51 NORTHUMBERLAND FUS.	
4 pm	B Coy under Capt G.O.H. FURNELL dug trenches to fill up a gap in MIDDLESEX line on right of ROYAL SCOTS	
6 pm	400 rounds of S.A.A. killed in a farm 100 about 500 yards in rear. Memo from Brigade Major to say that an attack in armed forced would be made for an advance at daybreak	

1247 W 3299 200,000 (E) 8/14 J.B.C. & A. Forms/C. 2118/11.

WAR DIARY
or
INTELLIGENCE SUMMARY.
(Erase heading not required.)

Army Form C. 2118

Hour, Date, Place	Summary of Events and Information	Remarks and references to Appendices
15 oct VIELLE CHAPELLE	Also stating that 15 portable footbridges had been sent up to the train, 5 of which were to be handed over to the Northumberland Fus^{rs}., these footbridges however, never reached the Battⁿ. Counter attack by Germans on our right flank during the night, repulsed by rifle fire.	
11. am	"B" Coy advanced slightly. 2/Lt W H FLINN wounded. ½ "C" Coy went up to reinforce "B" Coy. — The line of Battⁿ is as follows — GORDONS — Barricade from left right was as follows — GORDONS — ROYAL SCOTS — 1 Coy. MIDDLESEX ½ C Coy and "B" Coy ROYAL IRISH under Capt. G.O.M. FURNELL, 1 Coy MIDDLESEX	
11.30 am	Major Genl HAMILTON Com^{dg} 3rd Div. killed by Shrapnel bullet whilst standing on road opposite our trenches, following a debut K FOWLKES. Staff of 5 officers (Capt^s A.W.E.KNOX, C.A. FRENCH, J.A. SMITHWICK 4/18 and 2/Lieuts T. NICHOLSON Spec Res & R.G.H MOORE) and 353 men arrived returned in reserve	
1.0 pm	Our Artillery shelled the enemy's trenches (about 350 x infantry m.s.) to the village of St VAAST — the German Artillery replied by shelling our supports — the Battⁿ supports consisted of A Coy D ½ C Coy (there were only 3 coys after time)	
2.15 pm	The line advanced captured the enemy's trenches and drove them back through the village of St VAAST as far as the front of the bayonet	

WAR DIARY or INTELLIGENCE SUMMARY

Army Form C. 2118.

(Erase heading not required.)

Instructions regarding War Diaries and Intelligence Summaries are contained in F.S. Regs., Part II. and the Staff Manual respectively. Title pages will be prepared in manuscript.

Hour, Date, Place	Summary of Events and Information	Remarks and references to Appendices
18th Oct 1914 LE POUICKE 5. p.m.	For operation 8th Inf Bde for 18 Oct see APPENDIX XXII Batn standing to all day, heavy artillery fire in vicinity. For situation of 2nd Corps at dusk on 17th Oct see APPENDIX XXIII Orders received to support the French, advanced in direction of LE RIEZ and occupied the village with little opposition. Trifled in some large farm houses. The French were believed to be on our left. The 9th Bde held a line on our right through HERLIES. 14th Gp of 8th Inf Bde at AUBERS. The MIDDLESEX took up line of outposts N of held AUBERS by the Batn during night of 17th/18. Remainder of Brigade in reserve at AUBERS	APPENDIX XXII APPENDIX XXIII
9. p.m.	Kent Hadjt M.G. Section rifles & Grench line in front of the village. B, C & D Coys were ordered work all available tools dug themselves in as well as possible from left to right viz B.D.C. A Coy remained in reserve in the village with Regtl H Qrs. The French line was a ditch improvised. C Coy was slightly in rear of own line with its left firming back, At dawn digging ceased & rations were issued having been drawn from HERLIES. One platoon from B Coy plus plain from D Co were placed in support	
1.0 p.m. 18th Oct LE RIEZ 4 aux.		

WAR DIARY or INTELLIGENCE SUMMARY

(Erase heading not required.)

Army Form C. 2118.

Instructions regarding War Diaries and Intelligence Summaries are contained in F.S. Regs., Part II. and the Staff Manual respectively. Title pages will be prepared in manuscript.

Hour, Date, Place	Summary of Events and Information	Remarks and references to Appendices
4 a.m. 19th Oct 14 Le RIES	of the line behind a house about 60x in rear of the left of B Co. M.G. Detachment on right of "D" Co in advance of the house. The remainder of the Companies rested in the trenches. When the Patrols had taken Le RIES the Regl transport 1 S.A. Conts advanced to Le Plouich — Embryo Morning 19th Le Plouich was shelled, Ptn transport retired to AUBERS remainder there, the S.A. Conts stopped at Le Plouich	
2 p.m.	Our Artillery began to shell LE PILLY then enemy shelling our trenches	
3 p.m.	Both attacked and seized LE PILLY After dark Patrols dug themselves in Lieut LAING with M.G. detachment went back to outskirts of HERLIES and brought back all returns possible from our transport, wagons and sketch. See APPENDICES XXIV & XXV for details of attack	APPENDICES XXIV & XXV
LE PILLY 9 p.m.		
20 Oct 14 LE PILLY	Unfortunately little evidence is obtainable of what occurred on this day. — See APPENDICES XXVI and XXVII. An account by Lieut MARTEN 5 6th Active Regt German Army has also been obtained & added APPENDIX XXVIII. 19 & 20 Oct See APPENDIX XXIX for Casualties	APPENDICES XXVI and XXVII APPENDIX XXVIII APPENDIX XXIX

Army Form C. 2118.

WAR DIARY
or
INTELLIGENCE SUMMARY

(Erase heading not required.)

Instructions regarding War Diaries and Intelligence Summaries are contained in F. S. Regs., Part II. and the Staff Manual respectively. Title pages will be prepared in manuscript.

Hour, Date, Place	Summary of Events and Information	Remarks and references to Appendices
6.0.P.M. 24.10.14. ST OMER.	Arrived by motor buses and relieved - SUFFOLK REGT: for duty at G.H.Q. as Army Troops under S.O. Army Troops. The general state of the 131 men from Battalion on arrival as regards outfit and equipment was so bad as to be indescribable, there was not a sound pair of boots amongst them, equipment unserviceable and deficient and clothing unserviceable. No duty N.C.O's were amongst the party except the Scout and Machine Gun Sergeants the remainder of the N.C.O's were Staff Sergeants.	
25th October. 1914.	Major S.E.St.LEGER arrived from England and assumed command of the Battalion - A draft of 100 men also arrived under Command of CAPT RUDKIN. 2nd Battalion. The Infantry Barracks on arrival was in a most filthy condition, in most cases the men prefering to sleep in the open in shelters than occupy the barrack rooms, no institutions or conveniences of any kind for the comfort of the	

1247 W 3299 200,000 (E) 8/14 J.B.C. & A. Forms/C. 2118/11.

Army Form C. 2118.

WAR DIARY or INTELLIGENCE SUMMARY

(Erase heading not required.)

Instructions regarding War Diaries and Intelligence Summaries are contained in F. S. Regs., Part II. and the Staff Manual respectively. Title pages will be prepared in manuscript.

Hour, Date, Place	Summary of Events and Information	Remarks and references to Appendices
26th October to 29th October. 1914. ST. OMER.	Owing to the few men and the bad state of clothing and Equipment the Battalion was unable to perform the Garrison Duties as required to be furnished by G.H.Q.Troops. Only orderlies could be detailed. Commencement of process of ordering stores, equipment and clothing. Refitting, training N.C.O's and men to perform Ceremonial Guard also in duties in the Field.	
30th October. 1914.	Orders received from Adjutant General to re-organise the Bn: on a 2 Company Battalion Basis. The necessary personnel and war outfit was wired for to War Office. Necessary indents for clothing, equipment etc., sent by wire.	X: to be ready in a week
1st November. 1914.	Training of N.C.O's and men for duties in the field proceeded with.	
6.0.P.M. 2.11.1914.	Lieut W.H.S.BERRY. 4th ROYAL INNIS:FUS: and 100 men arrived as re-enforcement.	
3rd to 14th November 1914.	Routine work included drilling and training N.C.O's and men in Ceremonial Guard duties and also for service in the Field. The large majority of N.C.O's arriving with re-enforcements entirely ignorant of their duties in Peace and War.	
14th November. 1914.	34 draught animals and 15 vehicles received.	
15th November. 1914.	Furnished Guard of Honour to body of late FIELD MARSHAL EARL ROBERTS who died at this Station.	

Army Form C. 2118.

WAR DIARY
or
INTELLIGENCE SUMMARY
(Erase heading not required.)

Instructions regarding War Diaries and Intelligence Summaries are contained in F. S. Regs., Part II. and the Staff Manual respectively. Title pages will be prepared in manuscript.

Hour, Date, Place	Summary of Events and Information	Remarks and references to Appendices
St. OMER. 15th December.1914.	Battalion organized on 4 Company basis and Officers posted to Companies as follows. "A" Company. Captain. Dawson. Commanding. Lieut. Ward Simpson. 2nd Lieut.MacSweeney. "B" Company. Captain. Wickham. Commanding. Lieut. White. 2/Lt. Lowe. "C" Company. Captain Morrogh. Commanding. Lieut. Berry. 2/,, Blake. "D" Company. Captain. Brown. Commanding. 2nd Lieut.Phillips. ,, ,, McLoughlin.	
17th December.1914.	Major S.E.St.LEGER appointed Assistant Camp Comdt: G.H.Q. graded as D.A.A.G. Captain H.E.RUDKIN. assumed the duty of Senior Major of Battalion.	
21st December.1914.	Major R.G.S.MORIARTY assumed command of the Battalion vice MAJOR E.T.BUCKLEY to his unit.	

1247 W 3299 200,000 (E) 8/14 J.B.C. & A. Forms/C. 2118/11.

Army Form C. 2118.

WAR DIARY
or
INTELLIGENCE SUMMARY
(Erase heading not required.)

Instructions regarding War Diaries and Intelligence Summaries are contained in F. S. Regs., Part II. and the Staff Manual respectively. Title pages will be prepared in manuscript.

Hour, Date, Place	Summary of Events and Information	Remarks and references to Appendices
31st December. 1914. St. OMER.	2nd Lieuts J.S.LUCKETT. A.L.RAMSAY. W.P.HINTON. joined. For Offices who left during Dec. See APPENDIX XXXII	APPENDIX XXXII
12 Noon. 1st Jany: 1915. St OMER.	Battalion inspected by Commander-in-Chief Field Marshal Sir JOHN FRENCH - Colonel-in-Chief of the Regiment.	
8th January. 1915.	Draft - 117 N.C.O's and men and Lieut A.S.PIM joined.	
13th January. 1915.	Furnished Guard of Honour for PRESIDENT POINCARE.	
17th January. 1915.	Furnished Guard of Honour for GENERAL JOFFRE.	
18th January. 1915.	Draft 13 N.C.O's and 13 Drummers joined. LIEUT T.W.FITZPATRICK appointed Adjutant with effect from 21.10.14.	
20th January. 1915.	Captain C.A.FRENCH and Lieut & Qr.Mr. T.MAHONY and 75 N.C.O's and men joined.	

Army Form C. 2118.

WAR DIARY
or
INTELLIGENCE SUMMARY

(Erase heading not required.)

Instructions regarding War Diaries and Intelligence Summaries are contained in F. S. Regs., Part II. and the Staff Manual respectively. Title pages will be prepared in manuscript.

Hour, Date, Place	Summary of Events and Information	Remarks and references to Appendices
26th January. 1915 St. OMER.	His Eminence Cardinal BOURNE visited and addressed the Battalion.	
31st January. 1915	Furnished Guard of Honour for RUSSIAN AMBASSADOR.	

12

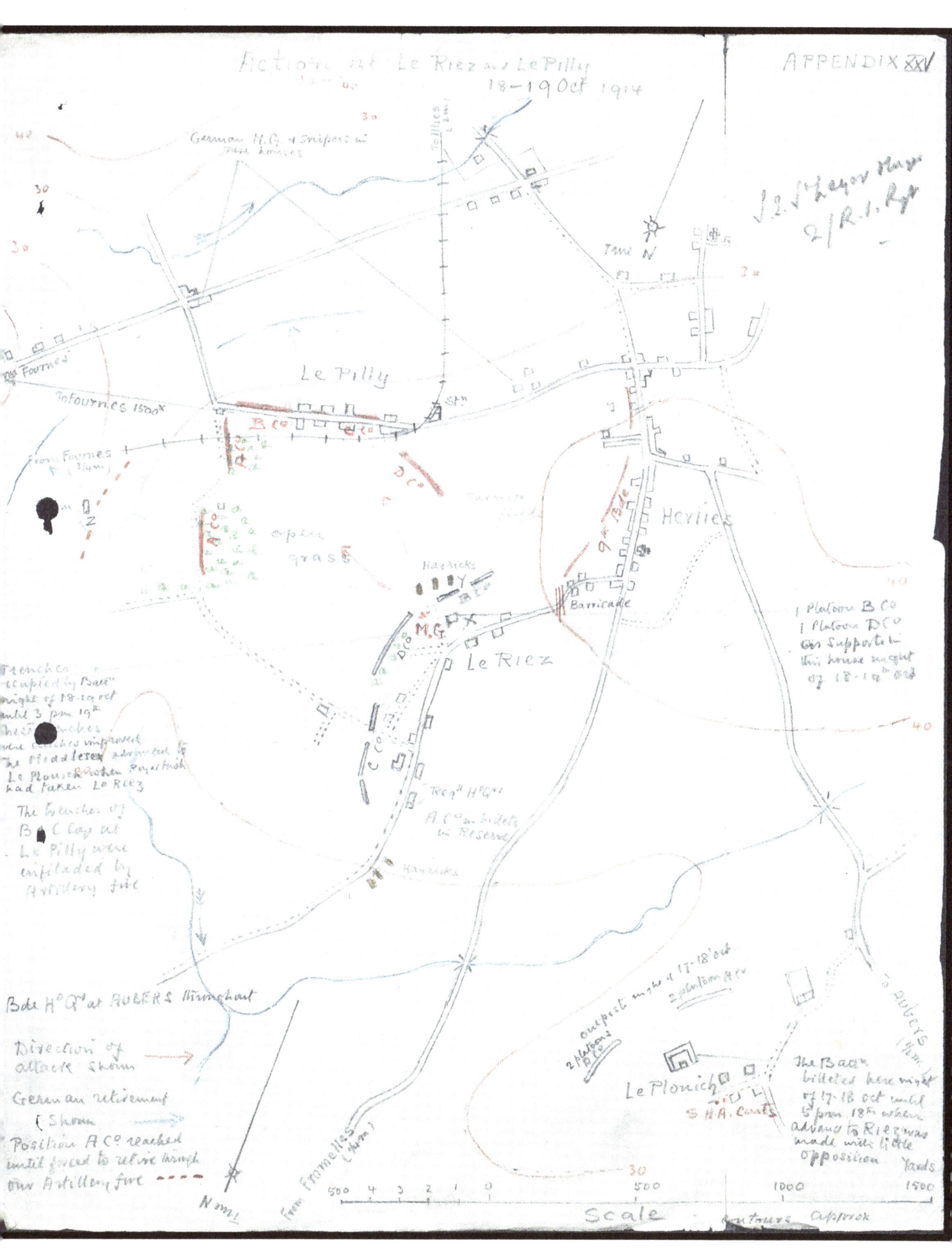

APPENDIX XXX

Army Form C. 2118.

WAR DIARY
or
INTELLIGENCE SUMMARY

(Erase heading not required.)

Instructions regarding War Diaries and Intelligence Summaries are contained in F. S. Regs, Part II. and the Staff Manual respectively. Title pages will be prepared in manuscript.

APPENDIX XXX

Hour, Date, Place	Summary of Events and Information	Remarks and references to Appendices
DENBIEN WERPUY 19 & 20 October 1915	The following Officers were present with the Battalion on the 19th - 20th October. 1915. **Head Quarters.** Major. E.H.Daniell. Commanding. Lieut M.C.C.Harrison. Adjt. Lieut. D.P.Laing. M.G.Officer. Lieut E.M.Phillips. T'port. Lieut. J.L.Jackson. R.A.M.C. Capt. Rawlinson. Chaplain. **"A" Company.** Capt. J.A.Smithwick. Commanding. Lieut.A.M.Tandy. Lieut.D.S.Smythe. **"B" Company.** Capt.G.O.M.Furnell. Commanding. Lieut.J.Ross-Smyth. Lieut.J.H.McLoughlin. Lieut.T.Nicholson. **"C" Company.** C.A.French. Captain ~~Kirkwood~~. Commanding. Lieut.K.Foulkes. Lieut.P.E.N.Howard. **"D" Company.** Captain. A.C.Knox. Commdg: Lieut. A.R.Newton King. Lieut. H.G.Downing. Lieut. H.G.Moore. **Draft.** Lieut W.E.Bredin. Lieut A.J.Anderson.	M

1247 W 3299 200,000 (E) 8/14 J.B.C. & A. Forms/C. 2118/11.

Army Form C. 2118.

WAR DIARY
or
INTELLIGENCE SUMMARY

(Erase heading not required.)

Instructions regarding War Diaries and Intelligence Summaries are contained in F. S. Regs., Part II. and the Staff Manual respectively. Title pages will be prepared in manuscript.

APPENDIX XXXI

Hour, Date, Place	Summary of Events and Information	Remarks and references to Appendices
	OFFICERS WHO JOINED 2ND BN. THE ROYAL IRISH REGIMENT DURING NOV: 1914.	
	Captain L.K.V. Brown, The Royal Irish Regiment 21.11.14.	
	Captain A. Gorham Royal Munster Fusiliers ,,	W
	Captain S.G. Smithwick Royal Dublin Fusiliers. ,,	
	Captain M. Wickham Connaught Rangers ,,	
	Lieut. O. Pemberton Royal Munster Fusiliers ,,	W
	,, R.O.C. Bush Royal Dublin Fusiliers. ,,	
	Captain J.D. Morrogh Royal Irish Regiment 8.11.14.	W
	Major E.P. Thompson Royal Munster Fusiliers 12.11.14.	W
	2/Lieut. M.C. MacSweeney Royal Dublin Fusiliers 13.11.14.	
	,, ,, J.P. McLoughlin ,, ,, ,,	
	Lieut. E.R.K. White ,, ,, ,,	
	2/Lieut. T/A. Lowe Royal Irish Fusiliers ,,	
	Lieut. J. Glascott North Staffordshire Regt. 15.11.14.	
	Captain G.S.T. Dawson Royal Irish Regiment 25.11.14.	
	Lieut. V.E. Ward Simpson ,, ,, ,,	
	Lieut. P. Walsh Royal Army Medical Corps 29.11.14.	W

1247 W 3299 200,000 (E) 8/14 J.B.C. & A. Forms/C. 2118/11.

APPENDIX XXXII

APPENDIX XXXII

Army Form C. 2118

WAR DIARY
or
INTELLIGENCE SUMMARY
(Erase heading not required.)

Instructions regarding War Diaries and Intelligence Summaries are contained in F. S. Regs., Part II. and the Staff Manual respectively. Title pages will be prepared in manuscript.

Hour, Date, Place	Summary of Events and Information	Remarks and References to Appendices
APPENDIX:-		
	OFFICERS WHO LEFT 2ND BN. THE ROYAL IRISH REGIMENT DURING DECEMBER, 1914.	
	Captain Rawlinson (Roman Catholic Chaplain) to Rouen 3.12.14.	
	Captain Gorham A. R.W.Fusiliers. To his unit 8.12.14.	
	,, Smithwick S.G. Royal D.Fus. ,, ,,	
	Lieut. Pemberton O. Royal M. Fus. ,, ,,	
	,, Bush R.O.C. Royal D. Fus. ,, ,,	
	Major Thompson E.P. Royal M. Fus. ,, 14/12.14.	
	Lt.Col. Buckley E.J. Royal Inn.Fus. ,, 21.12.14.	
	MAJOR S'LEGER S.E. Royal Irish Regt. Asst Camp Commandant General Head Quarters 17/12/14	

www.ingramcontent.com/pod-product-compliance
Lightning Source LLC
Chambersburg PA
CBHW081455160426
43193CB00013B/2493